Easy Embroidery on Paper

Joke de Vette

SEARCH PRESS

Contents

Acknowledgements

I want to thank the following for their contribution to this book: my husband Adriaan, for the text and help with the patterns; Sjaak van Went, for making and developing the patterns; Mrs C. Gorissen for her assistance; Sandra Broekhuizen and Marike den Brok, for the organisation and part of the design.
I am grateful to the following for providing photos: Frans van Maurik (photo of granddaughter); Tiny Bos (photo of grandmother with grandchild).

Materials

- pricking mat
- fine stylus (Pergamano single point)
- fine embroidery needles
- embroidery or sewing machine threads
- masking tape
- paper 170 to 250 g weight
- white paper inserts 120 g weight
- paperclips
- adhesive without water (e.g. photo adhesive or glue stick)
- copy of the pattern to be pricked out
- gel pen or ballpoint pen
- mechanical pencil 0.3 mm lead or HB pencil with a sharp point
- eraser
- optional sheet of thin foam
- optional cutting mat, knife with snap-off blade and ruler
- optional small gemstones in various colours

General method

Pattern

Copy the pattern from the book using a photocopier. Fix the cut-out pattern to the card with paperclips. You can also use masking tape. This works better than the normal adhesive tape because it can be removed easily afterwards.

Each pattern has a border to help you place the pattern accurately on the card. Most borders are smaller than the card. If you are using paperclips you will need to cut the pattern out larger, say as wide as the card. That makes it easier to fix the pattern to the card.

Pricking

Lay a sheet of foam on the pricking mat and the card on top of it with the pattern as the top layer. Using the foam means the holes will be more even. Use a fine stylus and hold it vertically. Try to prick all the holes as accurately as possible because that will make the work neater.

Do not make the holes too big because when you are doing the embroidery you will have to turn the card to see where you are working. If the holes are too large the needle will keep falling out of the card.

Embroidery

The cards in this book have been embroidered with Sulky threads, unless otherwise stated. The colours and the embroidery stitches are given for each card.

Finishing off

When the embroidery has been completed, the holes may still be visible, so after finishing the embroidery, rub the back of the card with a smooth rounded object to close the holes. A clean teaspoon is ideal.

Then glue the back of the embroidery to a white insert sheet. You can also glue the embroidered card to another card. Wipe away any photo adhesive on the border with your finger or a piece of cloth. You can remove dry adhesive with your finger or the tip of a rubber.

NB Limit skin contact with fresh adhesive because it can cause a reaction.

Embroidery stitches

The description of the embroidery stitches is perhaps different from what you are used to. I shall show you the various stitches to make it easier for you to embroider the designs without charts. Many stitches with different names look the same; only the shape is different because the holes are pricked to form a different pattern. The drawings show the basic stitch with a thick line. Repeats are drawn with a thin line.

Straight stitch

Straight stitch is simply a thread between two holes (not illustrated).

Running stitch

Running stitch is only used to embroider very fine lines or small loops, such as a small eye.

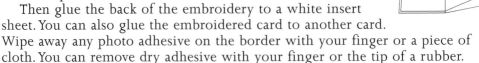
Running stitch

Bring the thread through the first hole from behind, take it through the next hole to the back, bring it to the front again through the third and so on. To make a solid line the stitches are worked first in one direction and then in the reverse one; see the diagram.

Stem stitch

Stem stitch is used for bigger details and somewhat thicker lines. Take the needle through the first hole in the line from back to front. Skip one hole and then take the thread through to the back of the card and go back one hole on the reverse. This is the basis of stem stitch. Keep repeating the basic stitch.

Stem stitch

Long stem stitch (simple)

Long stem stitch gives a line with a corded effect. It can be embroidered in two ways. The simple method has the same

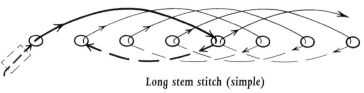

Long stem stitch (simple)

shape as plain stem stitch but there is a greater distance between the step forward and the step back. For example go five holes forward on the front of the card (1–5) and three holes back on the reverse. See the diagram.

The stitch can be much longer, for example going eight holes forward on the front of the work (1–9) and seven back on the reverse. A disadvantage of this method is that a lot of the thread is wasted on the back of the card.

Tip: with simple long stem stitch, don't count the holes on the back but just estimate the number.

Thin ends

The beginnings and ends of long stem stitch are often thin. Fill them in with a few short stitches. This applies to both versions of long stem stitch.

Extending and shortening long stem stitch

If you come to a short curve or you want a thinner line, shorten the long stem stitch. Make the backward stitch shorter and take the forward stitch to the first free hole. Continue with the new length of stitch. When you are past the curve or you want a thicker line, then lengthen the long stem stitch. Make the backward stitch longer and take the forward stitch to the first free hole. Continue with the new length of stitch. This method works for both versions of long stem stitch.

Tip: don't think about it too much. Just try to shorten and lengthen by eye. You'll soon get the hang of it.

Long stem stitch (normal)

This method gives the same corded effect as the simple one

Long stem stitch (normal)

but uses less thread. The diagram shows that on the front of the card you go back and forth with stitches of the same length but at the back of the card you only go forward one hole. Make the basic stitch, shown by a thick line, and go on repeating it. You can choose a longer or shorter stitch than shown in the diagram. The stitches on the back remain the same.

The stitches on the back help to keep the length of the stitches constant. With a stitch length of 1–5, 1–7, 1–9 and so on, the stitches on the back form a solid line (this does not apply to the first pair of stitches).

Circle stitch

Circle stitch is like long stem stitch (normal), but is easier to work because you can see what you are doing. The diagram makes it clear straight away. Embroider

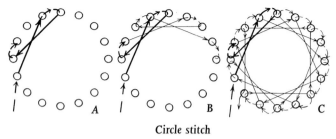

Circle stitch

on the front of the card with even long stitches back and forth. On the back always make a small stitch, just one hole forward. The stitches on the back always go in the same direction. Draw an arrow on the back to prevent mistakes.

Starting at any hole, count the required number of holes once and take the thread to the back. Complete the basic stitch, shown by a thick line without counting, as in diagram A. Repeat the basic stitch without counting until the circle is complete. There will be two threads in each hole, as shown in diagrams B and C.

You can also work with circle stitch with shorter or longer stitches.

Filling in stitch

Filling in stitch is a special type of circle stitch. You can completely fill in circles, stars and so on.

The first stitch goes through the centre to the front and then to the other side of the figure. There must be an equal number of holes to left and right of the first stitch, otherwise things will not work out.

Work the basic stitch, shown with a thick line, and repeat until the figure has been filled in. All the stitches on the back go in the same direction. Before you begin, draw an arrow on the reverse. This will prevent mistakes.

Filling in stitch

Fan stitch

Fan stitch is used for filling in flower petals and similar figures. You can also use it to fill in a circle. The central

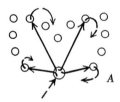
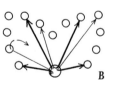

Fan stitch

hole must clearly be made larger than the other holes.

Bring the thread to the front through the central hole. Take it to the back at the edge of the figure and again through the central hole to the front. This is the basis of fan stitch. Repeat the stitch until the figure is filled in.

Try to avoid crossing the threads as follows: with each thread that you take from the centre to the edge, you miss several holes, as in diagram A; when you reach the end of the figure, embroider a thread in each opening, as in diagram B; after, say, the fourth round, the whole figure will be filled in, as in diagram C.

Filling stitch

Filling stitch fills in the space between two lines. The lines may meet at one end but they do not have to. The stitches are not always of the same length, but they are worked in the same way as in circle stitch. When the lines across have been worked, embroider the outlines along the row of holes.

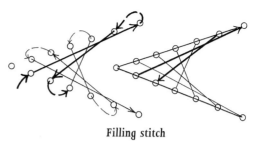

Filling stitch

Loop stitch

Loop stitch resembles fan stitch but it is more suitable for larger figures. The threads in loop stitch should barely cross each other, to give a prettier effect, and so that you waste less thread on the back of the card.

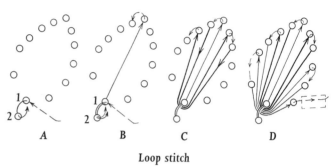

Loop stitch

Begin by making a loop, as in diagrams A and B. Bring the thread to the front through hole 1 and back through hole 2. Repeat once more. That forms a double loop.

Now bring the thread through the first hole for a third time and go back through the middle hole at the edge of the figure – this is often indicated by an arrow on the pattern. Stitch behind to a hole on the left or right of it. In diagram C the V-shaped basic stitches are shown by thick lines. Make these stitches. Only go through to the back of the card at the edge of the figure. At the loop, simply lay the needle almost flat on the paper and slide it under the loop. Next time, go under the loop in the opposite direction. In that way you avoid threads crossing each other. Repeat the basic stitch until the figure is complete, as in diagram D.

Zigzag stitch

At first zigzag stitch seems rather strange. This is because on the front of the card we do not go forwards but back at a slight angle. On the back, though, we do always move on one hole.

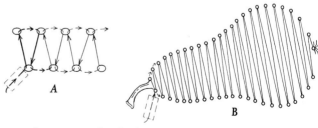

Work zigzag stitch between two lines on which there are (almost) the same number of holes. The lines can be of any shape.
In diagram A, two stitches are shown – these form the basis of the zigzag stitch. Repeat these stitches until the whole figure has been filled in; see diagram B.

Be careful! To make a good start the first stitch usually has to run back at an angle. Find the correct hole with which to begin (see diagram A).

Cross stitch

There are at least three good methods of working cross stitch. That shown is the same as for arrow stitch. Each cross stitch is completed before moving on to the next one.

Cross stitch

Arrow stitch

Arrow stitch is suitable for filling the space between two lines with a pretty pattern. The space may be wide, as in a candle, but also narrow, as for the stem of a flower. Below you can see a narrow arrow stitch from 1 to 3 and a somewhat broader one from 1 to 4. The stitch can also be made much wider.

The basis of arrow stitch is ordinary cross stitch; see diagram A. Keep repeating the stitch until the figure is complete. Diagram B shows that the second cross stitch overlaps the first. As you continue to embroider you get the desired arrow pattern, shown in diagram C; to complete the pattern you work a few extra stitches, as in diagram D.

It is actually better to begin with the extra stitches and then work the arrow stitch itself.

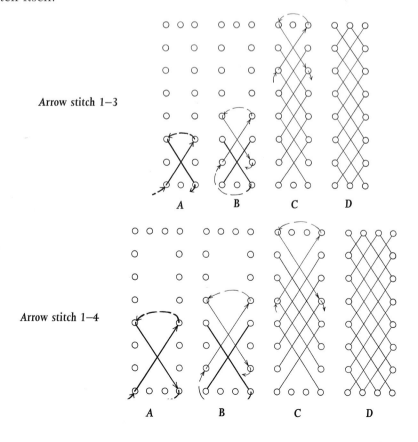

Arrow stitch 1–3

Arrow stitch 1–4

A B C D

A B C D

Tilting aperture cards

The flower patterns in this chapter are intended for the embroidering of tilting aperture cards, but they can equally well be used to make ordinary cards. After doing the embroidery you can add extra effects with small gemstones. For the stitches see the General method on page 3.

How do you use tilting aperture cards?

A tilting aperture card is made up of two parts: a double card and a single card. The double card has an oval punched in it. You can remove this carefully from the card. The single card has a larger oval punched that you can also remove from the card. The embroidery is worked on that oval. When the embroidery is complete you stick the smaller oval onto the back of the work. Prick and embroider a border pattern round the opening of the double card. You can swap the border patterns around. Use the border of the single card to cover the back of the embroidery on the double card.

   When the embroidery is ready, slip the embroidered oval into the slots in the double card. The inserted oval will not fall out, but can be tilted.

How do you work with an ordinary card?

First prick the border pattern along the borders of the ordinary card. Then lay the flower pattern in the middle and prick it into the card. If you put the card on a light box or hold it against a window, you can see the holes of the border pattern through the paper of the flower pattern. Use masking tape or similar to attach the flower pattern to the middle of the card. You can use the pieces of tape more than once.

Light green card (bottom left, page 11)

The flower pattern is 1A and the border pattern 1E (page 10).

   Embroider the green leaves with loop stitch, the circle with circle stitch and the tiny flowers at the top with filling in stitch. Use long stem stitch for the rest; the stitch length is mainly 1–5; see the General method. The threads to use are Sulky gold 7007, green 7018, red 7014, purple 7050 and pink 7012. A few gemstones will make your card extra special.

1A

Light green card (top right, page 11)

The flower pattern is 1B and the corner pattern is 1F.

The round flower on the left is embroidered with filling in stitch; for the others use fan stitch. The flower stem can be worked in arrow stitch. Use (long) stem stitch for the rest. For the corner patterns use fan stitch and long stem stitch.

The threads are Sulky gold 7007, green 7018, red 7041 and mixed red-gold-green 7027. Several gemstones have been added to the example shown.

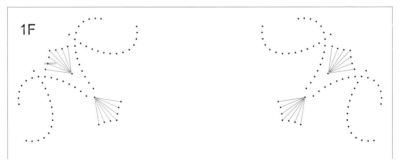

Pink card with large flower (top left, page 11)

The flower pattern is 1C and the border pattern 1G (both on page 12). The circles in the corner have been worked with circle stitch 1–7. The ovals are worked in circle stitch 1–5. The curves in the corner are worked with long stem stitch 1–5. Stop at each corner and begin again.

The flower motif is worked in long stem stitch; for short lines and small curves use short stitches; for longer lines use longer stitches.

Use Sulky threads
gold 7007, olive
green 7056 and
purple 7050. You
can stick a few
gemstones in the
flower and in
the corners.

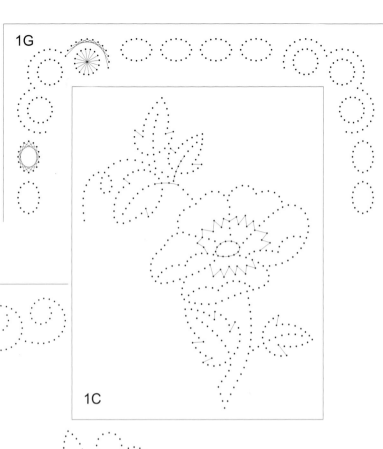

1G

1C

1D

Pink card with two flowers (bottom right, page 11)

The pattern is 1D. First prick
the flower motif and the left-
hand border pattern. Draw the
flower motif in pencil, then
turn the pattern over and prick
the right-hand border pattern.

Embroider the green leaf
above the flowers with loop
stitch. You can use circle stitch
or filling stitch for the small
circles. This also applies to the
ovals along the border. Use long
stem stitch for the rest.

Use Sulky threads gold 7007,
olive green 7056, purple 7050
and pink 7012. Some small
gemstones in the flowers and
the corners will make the card
look even more festive.

New baby cards

This chapter shows four very different cards, from bright and breezy to cuddly and cute, yet they are all suitable for new baby cards.

You will find diagrams and descriptions for the embroidery stitches used in the General method on page 3.

Stick the eyes on or ink them in

The eyes on these cards are small. You can use a gemstone but it must be no more than 2mm. Inking in the eyes using a ballpoint pen or a gel pen is another good solution, but let the ink dry properly before you begin to embroider because any kind of ink can leave spots on your work.

Embossing

Three cards have embossing in the corners. You could also use your own choice of decoration.

Mother and child

Prick pattern 2A into the card and ink in the eyes (see above). Embroider the eyes and the mouth with several running stitches. The rest is embroidered using stem stitch for the fine lines and long stem stitch for the thicker ones. For example, for the hair use a stitch length of 1–5 and for the lower curved line a stitch length of 1–7, to give a strong line.

The threads are Sulky gold 7007, pink 7012, light copper 7011 for the baby's hair and light blue 7052.

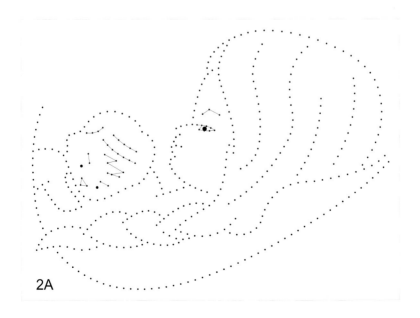

2A

Parachutist

Prick the pattern 2B into the card and ink in the eyes (see p.13). For the face use several straight stitches. Embroider the rest using stem stitch for details such as the hands and long stem stitch 1–5 for the rest.

The threads are Sulky silver 7001, copper 7010, pink 7012, blue 7016 and mixed silver-light copper-blue 7028.

Baby on a milk churn

Is the baby hungry or is he just in a hurry to put on weight? Prick pattern 2C into the card. There are no eyes to ink in. Embroider the fine details with short stitches and the thicker lines with long stem stitch 1–5. Use Sulky threads silver 7001, copper 7010 for the hair and the mouth, pink 7012 as the skin colour.

Teddy bear (top right, page 15)

The bear can be embroidered on a small card or on a large one with the decorative border. Prick pattern 2D (page 16) into the card and ink in the eye (see the beginning of this chapter).

Embroider the border with blue 7016 in long stem stitch 1–5. Stop at each corner and start again. You can embroider the small circles with stem stitch or filling in stitch.

2B

2C

2D

On the example shown, they have not been embroidered but yellow gemstones have been stuck on instead.

    Embroider the bear with light copper 7011 in stem stitch and long stem stitch; choose copper 7010 for the sole of the foot and use circle stitch 1–5. The ribbon is also embroidered in stem stitch and long stem stitch, using light blue 7052.

Out of doors

If these embroidered cards (page 19) are to be believed, animals are just as mad about outdoor activities as we are.

For the embroidery stitches see the General method on page 3.

Stick the eyes on or ink them in

One of the sample cards has wobbly eyes stuck on. You can also draw them in. Prick one or two holes for each eye. Then ink them in before you begin the embroidery, but let the ink dry properly, because all types of ink can leave spots on your work.

Our little fisherman

Prick pattern 3A into the card. You can ink in the eyes after pricking the design. A number of cross stitches are worked in the float. Embroider the picnic basket with straight stitches. Stem stitch is used for the small details and long stem stitch for the thicker lines.

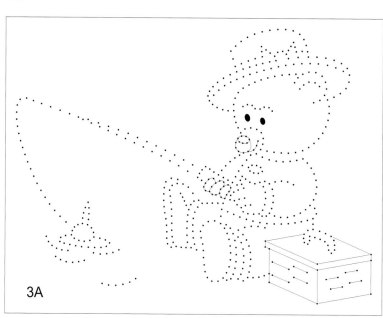

3A

The many colours liven up the picture. The threads used are Sulky copper 7010, light copper 7011, red 7014, green 7018, mixed silver-black 7023, purple 7050 and light blue 7053.

Camping

Our teddy bear finds camping great fun with a pot of honey and a big piece of cake.

Prick pattern 3B (page 18) in the card. You can then draw in the eyes. Embroider the straight lines – see the pricking pattern – with straight stitches. Use straight stitches for the eyebrows. Embroider the rest with stem stitch for the small details and long stem stitch for the thicker lines. Using a number of colours livens up the picture.

The threads are Sulky gold 7007, blue 7016, green 7018, mixed red-gold-green 7027, mixed silver-light copper-blue 7028 and olive green 7056.

The hedgehog

Our hedgehog stands on a tree stump like a ringmaster at the circus.
Prick pattern 3C (page 20) into the card. See the instructions above about sticking on or inking in the eyes.

The border is embroidered with filling stitch; always stitch over the lines of holes last. The braces have an infill of cross stitches; for the prickles and the lower part of the tree trunk use zigzag stitch. Use two straight stitches for the eyebrow and for the rest use stem stitch and long stem stitch.

The Sulky threads are copper 7010, light copper 7011, green 7018, mixed silver-black 7023 and red-gold-green 7027.

A dozen green 3 mm gemstones are stuck on the border.

3C

Swinging snakes

Our snakes on page 23 are busy with very human activities and concerns, rather than just hanging down over tree trunks in the jungle.

For the embroidery stitches used see the General method on page 3.

Stick the eyes on or ink them in

On two of the sample cards wobbly eyes have been stuck on. You could also ink in the eyes. When you prick the design, prick two holes for the eyes. Ink them in before you begin the embroidery, but let the ink dry properly, because all types of ink can leave spots on your work.

4A

Madam snake reads the cards

Prick pattern 4A into the card.

Embroider the necklace, eyes and earrings with circle stitch. For small details choose straight stitch or stem stitch and embroider the rest with long stem stitch. Circle stitch and long stem stitch (normal) are worked in the same way. The diagrams of the stitches are different but the instructions for each one are the same. See the General method on pages 5 and 6.

Use Sulky threads gold 7007, pink 7012, black 7051, red 7014, silver-black 7023 and purple 7050. You can decorate the necklace with various gemstones or small beads.

Snakes in love

The two snakes are looking deep into each other's eyes and they make a heart shape; a romantic fantasy.

Prick pattern 4B (page 22) into the card and take great care with the arrow shapes on the backs of the snakes. The whole card is embroidered in stem stitch.

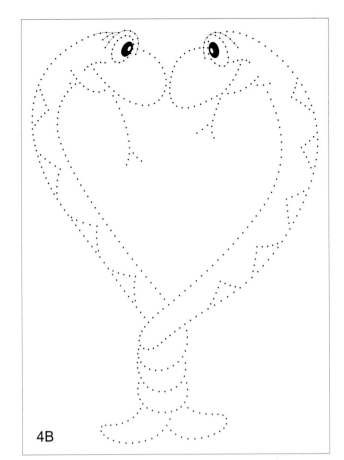

Use Sulky threads
gold 7007, red
7014 and
green 7018.

4B

4C

Mister snake is trying to make an impression

Prick pattern 4C
into the card.
Except for the
teeth, the whole
card is worked in
stem stitch and
long stem stitch.
Use small stitches
for the short lines
and longer stitches
for the longer lines.
The threads are
Sulky red 7014,
black 7051 for the
eyes, nose and
teeth, mixed
green-purple 7022
for the rest.

Flower cards

You will find the diagrams and instructions for the embroidery stitches used on these cards in the General method at the beginning of the book.

Square card (top, page 27)

The cream card shown is 132 mm (5¼ in) square. Prick pattern 5A into the card.

Embroider the wavy borders on the left and the lower edge of the card with long stem stitch 1–5. Stop at each corner and start again. Do the same with the outline of the rosette in the corner. The small circles inside the rosette are worked in circle stitch. The stitch length on the example is 1–6. Use fan stitch to embroider the rose shapes along the border.

Use fan stitch for the stripes in the flowers and embroider the outline of the flowers and the green with long stem stitch 1–5 or 1–6.

5A

The threads are Sulky gold 7007, pink 7012, purple 7050 and green 7018. Add a few gemstones to the rosette.

Arum lily (bottom left, page 27)

Prick pattern 5B into the card. Embroider the figure eights with long stem stitch 1–4 or 1–5. The small circles within these shapes can be worked with circle stitch or filling stitch. On the sample card they have been pricked but not embroidered. They have been filled in with 3 mm gemstones.

The flower stem can be embroidered in arrow stitch 1–4; see the beginning of this on the chart on this page. In the example the stamen of one flower has been worked in cross stitch and the other in arrow stitch. Embroider the rest of the pink and green in long stem stitch 1–5.

5B

The threads are Sulky gold 7007, pink 7012, black 7051 for the stamens and green 7018.

Thistles (bottom right, page 27)

Prick pattern 5C into the card. Embroider the green leaves and the fans in the corners in fan stitch. You can use your imagination to make the flowers and the flower stem out of arrow stitch, which fills them in nicely. The hairs on the flowers are self-explanatory. Work the rest in long stem stitch 1–5.

Use Sulky threads gold 7007, purple 7050 in the corners, olive green 7056 and mixed red-gold-green 7027. One 3 mm gemstone is placed in each of the four corners.

5C

Abstract shapes

Abstract shapes are generally straightforward to embroider because it is easy to see what you are doing. You don't really need to know the usual embroidery stitches. The shapes are very varied and you can experiment with different colours. A well-designed shape gives plenty of scope for fun with lines.

Fun with lines in green and gold (bottom right, page 31)

Prick model 7A into the card. Using a ruler as a guide will give straighter lines and a nicer shape. The green part consists of four groups of threads: see the indications on the pricking pattern. Using the order shown on this pattern will work best. Begin to embroider with threads from A to E, from E2 to A2, from A3 to E3 and so on. Do the same with B to E, C to E and D to E. Embroider the corners as shown from B to C and from D to A. Finally embroider the threads that cover the rows of holes; do this twice. The threads to use are Sulky gold 7007 and olive green 7056.

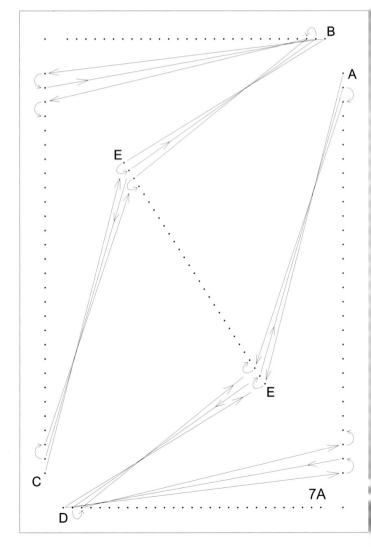

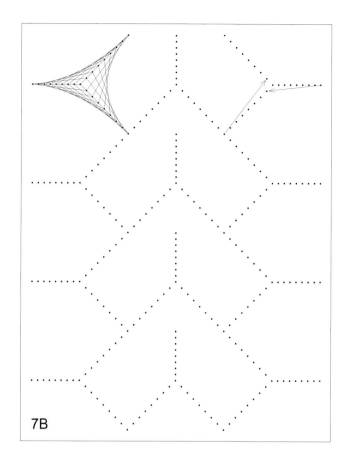

7B

Fun with triangles (top right, page 31)

Prick pattern 7B into the card.

Use filling stitch (see General method on page 7) to fill in the triangles. The stitch is worked three times for each triangle, twice with purple and once with gold. Begin embroidering each triangle with the thread that is shown above and to the right on the pattern. Work all the threads that cross in purple and gold, but do not work any threads that cover the rows of holes. When all the triangles have been completed, embroider the stitches that cover the rows of holes.

Use Sulky threads gold 7007 and purple 7050.

7C

Fun with circles (bottom left, page 31)

Prick pattern 7C into the card. Embroider the circles with circle stitch. The example was worked with a stitch length of 1–11, that is from 1 to 11. You could choose another length of stitch. Pattern 7C shows 1–9.

Embroider the straight lines with fan stitch. The central hole of each fan is shown on the pattern by a small circle; make this larger than the normal holes. Try to avoid crossing threads, see the General method on page 6. Finally work the stitches that cover the rows of holes.

Use Sulky threads green 7015, pink 7012 and mixed green-purple 7022.

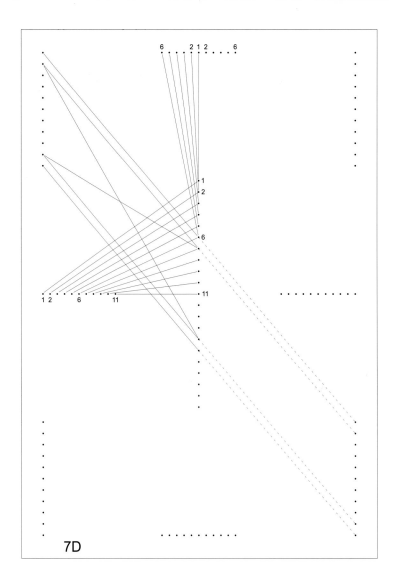

7D

Fun with lines (top left, page 31)

Prick pattern 7D into the card and look at the indications that are shown on the pattern. First of all embroider the groups of threads numbered 1, 2 and so on. Begin at the left with the horizontal line starting at point 1. Work from point 1 on the left to 1 on the vertical line, from point 2 next to it to 2 on the left and so on. Work in the same way below the horizontal line. Be careful: in hole number 11 of the horizontal line there should only be one thread.

Next embroider from point 1 on the vertical line to 1 on the upper edge of the card, from point 2 to 2 and so on. Embroider in the same way to the right of the vertical line but be careful: in hole 1 of the vertical line there should only be one thread.

Now give the card a half turn and embroider in the same way again. Finally work the straight crossing threads which lie diagonally across the card and also the stitches that cover the rows of holes.

Use Sulky threads gold 7007, olive green 7056 and red 7054.

Flowers on gift cards

All these flower patterns (on page 35) can be embroidered on small cards. If you mount the card on a slightly larger one in a suitable colour, your embroidery will look much better.

Gemstones

The cards are decorated with some gemstones. Most of them are 2 mm in diameter and you will find plenty of colours to choose from. You can be very generous with them.

Card with a red bow (top left, page 35)

The pattern is 6A. Embroider the flowers in fan stitch. Choose either circle stitch or filling in stitch for the tiny flowers. You can adapt arrow stitch for the main stem. Work the rest in long stem stitch.

   The threads are Sulky gold 7007, green 7018 and pink 7012, with purple 7050 in the heart of the flowers. You can add extra effects with gemstones.

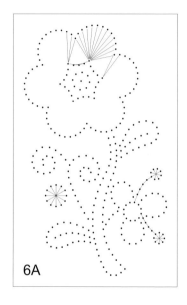

6A

6B

Card with yellow and green ribbon (bottom right, page 35)

The pattern is 6B. Embroider the whole pattern in long stem stitch. Use Sulky threads gold 7007, green 7018 and pink 7012 in the heart of the flowers.

Card with red ribbon
(bottom left, page 35)

The pattern is 6C. Embroider the heart of each flower with circle stitch and the rest with long stem stitch.

The threads are Sulky green 7018, red 7014, pink 7012 and purple 7050. Using some gemstones will make your embroidery sparkle.

6C

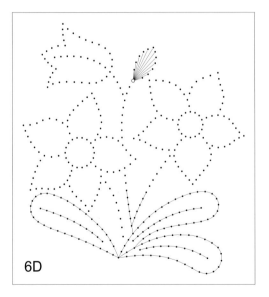

6D

Card with yellow and green ribbon
(top right, page 35)

For pattern 6D use circle stitch for the heart of the flowers and fan stitch for the small green leaf. Work the rest in stem stitch.

The Sulky threads are green 7018, light blue 7052 and dark blue 7016. You can brighten up the embroidery even more with small gemstones.

Jolly clowns

See the General method at the beginning of the book for diagrams and explanation of the embroidery stitches.

Stick the eyes on or ink them in

One of the cards has a large eye stuck on. The eyes are inked in on the others. When you prick the design on the card, prick one or two small holes for each eye. Ink in the eyes before you begin to embroider, but let the ink dry properly, because all types of ink can leave spots on your work.

Clown on a bicycle (bottom, page 39)

Prick pattern 8A into the card. Stick on the eye or ink it in as described above. Embroider the circles in circle stitch using various colours and different

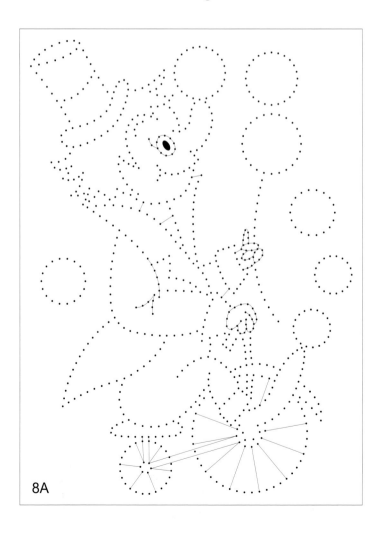

8A

lengths of stitch, to give variety. Circle stitch is also used for the bicycle wheels, with a stitch length of 1–7 for the front wheel and 1–5 for the back wheel. Embroider the straight lines as shown in the pattern. The bicycle can be embroidered in arrow stitch, or in long stem stitch. Use running stitch for the hands, stem stitch for the eyes and choose long stem stitch for the rest.

Use Sulky yarn silver 7001 for the wheels, copper 7010, red 7014, blue 7016, green 7018, black 7051 and mixed silver-black 7023 for the jacket and hat.

8B

Clown with a violin (top left, page 39)

The pattern is 8B. The card in the example has been coloured in with a watercolour pencil after the pricking. Stick the eyes on or ink them in as described on page 36.

Choose your own colour scheme for the embroidery on the card. Embroider the straight lines as shown in the pattern. The pompoms on the shoes are worked in circle stitch 1–5. For the rest, use stem stitch for the fine details and long stem stitch for the longer lines. A few gemstones will work wonders.

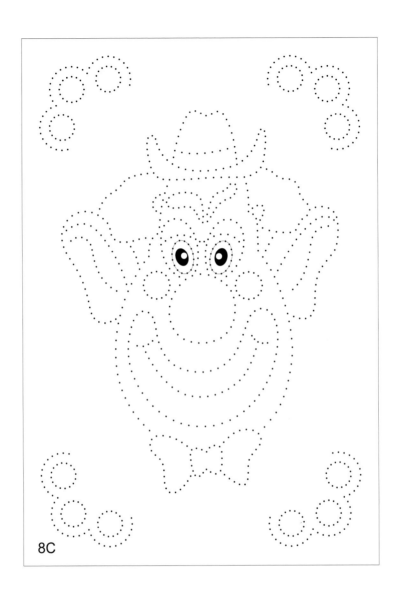

8C

Clown's head (top right, page 39)

Prick pattern 8C into the card. Then colour the card with watercolour pencil.
The large eyes shown in the photo have been stuck on. You could also colour
in the eyes; see the paragraph at the start of this chapter. The motifs in the
corners are worked with filling in stitch for the circles and long stem stitch for
the curves. Stop at each corner and start again. You can embroider the whole of
the clown's head in long stem stitches of different lengths, using short stitches
for short lines and bigger stitches for the longer ones.

The threads are Sulky pink 7012, red 7014, green 7018, mixed silver-black
7023 and mint green 7053.

Favourite photos

In this chapter there are three embroidered frames that will suit photos of different sizes. You can therefore choose the most suitable one for your photo. The size of the photo is drawn on each pattern.

For the embroidery stitches see the General method on page 3.

First of all select the best part of your photo. Make a photocopy of the pattern – preferably on 120 g weight paper – and cut out the inner circle with nail scissors following the line exactly. Lay the paper on the photo and move it around until you have found the best part. Using a ballpoint pen, draw round the edge of the opening, remove the pattern from the photo and cut the circle out of the photo very carefully. A bit of practice works wonders. A circle cutter without a centre point is a good tool.

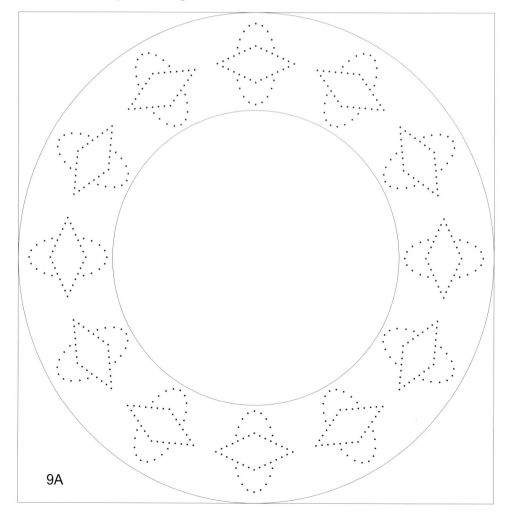

9A

Don't worry about cutting off a lot of the photo; one good detail is better than two or three very ordinary ones. A lot was cut off the photos in the examples. The flower photo is a detail from a bouquet that I was given on my 65th birthday.

Choose the colours of the threads and any gemstones to tone with the colours in the photo; for example red thread highlights the red parts of the photo. You can cover the embroidery on the back, but sticking the embroidered card on a larger one in a suitable colour gives a pretty effect.

Child with candle and grandmother with grandchild

The curves are worked in long stem stitch 1–4. Choose filling stitch for the triangular shapes. To cover the row of holes on the triangles, use either of the two colours. The small gemstones are available from art and craft suppliers.

9B

See the General method at the beginning of the book for diagrams and instructions for the embroidery stitches.

Flower card

All the curves on this card are worked in long stem stitch. You can choose either 1–7 or 1–5 for the stitch length. A stitch length of 1–7 is drawn on the pattern but 1–5 was used on the embroidered example. You can fill in the space between the bent ends of the motifs with one or two short stitches.

   The embroidered frame is made extra special with gemstones in the same colours as the threads.

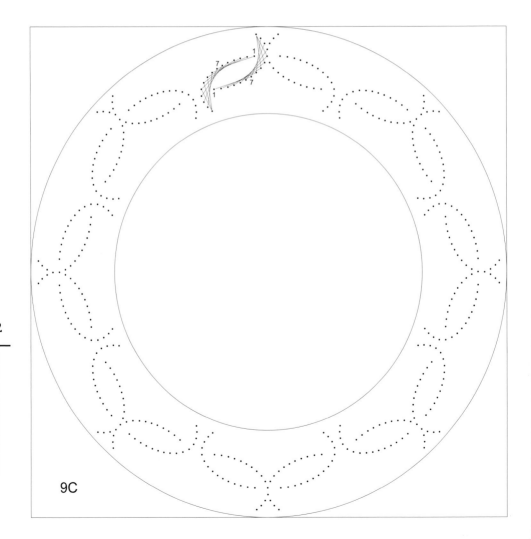

9C

Christmas wonderland

You can ink in the eyes and other black details on the cards on page 47. When you prick the pattern into the card, prick two holes for each eye. Draw the eyes and any other black details before you begin the embroidery and let them dry properly, because all types of ink can leave spots on your work. The diagrams and instructions for the stitches are at the front of the book.

Father Christmas
Very small gemstones are used for his eyes. Alternatively you could ink them in; see above.

10A

Prick pattern 10A into the card. Embroider the green of the eyes and eyebrows with stem stitch 1–3. Use a stitch length of 1–3 or 1–4 for the curls of the beard. Work the rest in long stem stitch 1–5. For the pompom on the hood, use circle stitch with a stitch length of 1–9 or 1–11. Fill in the thin ends with short stitches.

The Sulky threads used are silver 7001, pink 7012 and red 7014.

Tiny gemstones are stuck on the hood and in the corners. You could also use small beads or golden dots left over from sheets of stickers.

Lambs

Two lambs are looking at a special star. Could it be the star in the story of the first Christmas? Prick pattern 10B into the card. Ink in the noses and hooves in black; see instructions above.

Embroider the lambs in (long) stem stitch 1–3 or 1–4. Stop at each corner and begin again. Fill in very thin lines with a few short stitches.

The star is worked in fan stitch. The eight holes in the centre and the eight outer holes are used one by one as the central hole for a fan stitch. Make these holes larger than the others.

The thread is Sulky gold 7007 and light bronze 7011. In the open space you can stick a few gemstone stars or star-shaped stickers.

10B

45

Christmas kitten

Is this little kitten trying to have a snooze in Santa's boot?
Prick pattern 10C (page 46) into the card. Embroider the very thin lines in stem stitch 1–3 and the rest in long stem stitch 1–5.

The threads are Sulky silver 7001, pink 7012, red 7014, green 7018 and black 7051.

A few small gemstones will make the card even more attractive.

10C

Teddy bear with lantern

Prick pattern 10D (page 48) into the card. See the beginning of the chapter for the method of inking in the eyes.

Embroider the straight lines – see the pricking pattern – with long straight stitches. Repeat the stitches for the pole two or three times to make it thicker. Use circle stitch 1–5 for the pompom on the woolly hat and 1–4 for the nose. Embroider the mouth in stem stitch and the rest in long stem stitch 1–5.

The threads are Sulky light copper 7011, copper 7010, red 7014 for the lantern, green 7018 and mixed red-gold-green 7027.

A few gemstones or star-shaped stickers will liven up the card even more.

10D

First published in Great Britain 2007 by Search Press Limited
Wellwood, North Farm Road, Tunbridge Wells, Kent TN2 3DR

Reprinted 2007, 2008, 2010, 2012

Originally published in the Netherlands 2005 by
Cantecleer, an imprint of Tirion Uitgevers bv

English translation by Mary Boorman in association with
First Edition Translations Ltd, Cambridge

English translation copyright © Search Press Limited, 2007

English edition typeset by GreenGate Publishing Services, Tonbridge, Kent
Printed in Malaysia by Times Offset (M) Sdn Bhd

ISBN: 978 1 84448 195 8

Please visit the Search Press website for details of suppliers: www.searchpress.com